Citizenship

Being Fair

Cassie Mayer

Heinemann Library
Chicago, Illinois

© 2008 Heinemann Library
a division of Capstone Global Library, LLC.
Chicago, Illinois

Customer Service 888-454-2279
Visit our website at www.heinemannraintree.com

All rights reserved. No part of this publication may be reproduced or transmitted in any form or by any means, electronic or mechanical, including photocopying, recording, taping, or any information storage and retrieval system, without permission in writing from the publisher.

Designed by Joanna Hinton-Malivoire
Illustrated by Mark Beech

The Library of Congress has cataloged the first edition of this book as follows:
Mayer, Cassie.
Being fair / Cassie Mayer.
p. cm. -- (Citizenship)
Includes bibliographical references and index.
ISBN 978-1-4034-9483-2 (hc) -- ISBN 978-1-4034-9491-7 (pbk.) 1. Fairness--Juvenile literature. I. Title.
BJ1533.F2M39 2007
179'.9--dc22
2006039378

Printed in the United States 5576

Contents

What Does Being Fair Mean? 4
Ways to Be Fair 6
Activity 22
Picture Glossary 23
Index 24

Being fair means thinking of other people.

Being fair means treating people well.

When you share your toys ...

you are being fair.

When you wait your turn ...

you are being fair.

When you give someone else
a turn ...

you are being fair.

When you share a snack
with friends ...

you are being fair.

When you ask others to join in ...

you are being fair.

When you let others choose what to play ...

you are being fair.

When you think of how
others feel ...

you are being fair.

Being fair is important.

How can you be fair?

Activity

How is this child being fair?

Picture Glossary

fair agreeable for everyone

share to let someone else use what you have; to give someone else a part of what you have

Index

ask, 14
share, 6, 7, 12, 13
snack, 12, 13
take turns, 8, 9, 10, 11

Note to Parents and Teachers
Each book in this series shows examples of behavior that demonstrate good citizenship. Take time to discuss each illustration and ask children to identify the fair behavior shown. Use the question on page 21 to ask students how they can be fair in their own lives.

The text has been chosen with the advice of a literacy expert to enable beginning readers success while reading independently or with moderate support. You can support children's nonfiction literacy skills by helping them use the table of contents, picture glossary, and index.